I SPY

Valentine's Day

HAPPY
Valentine's Day

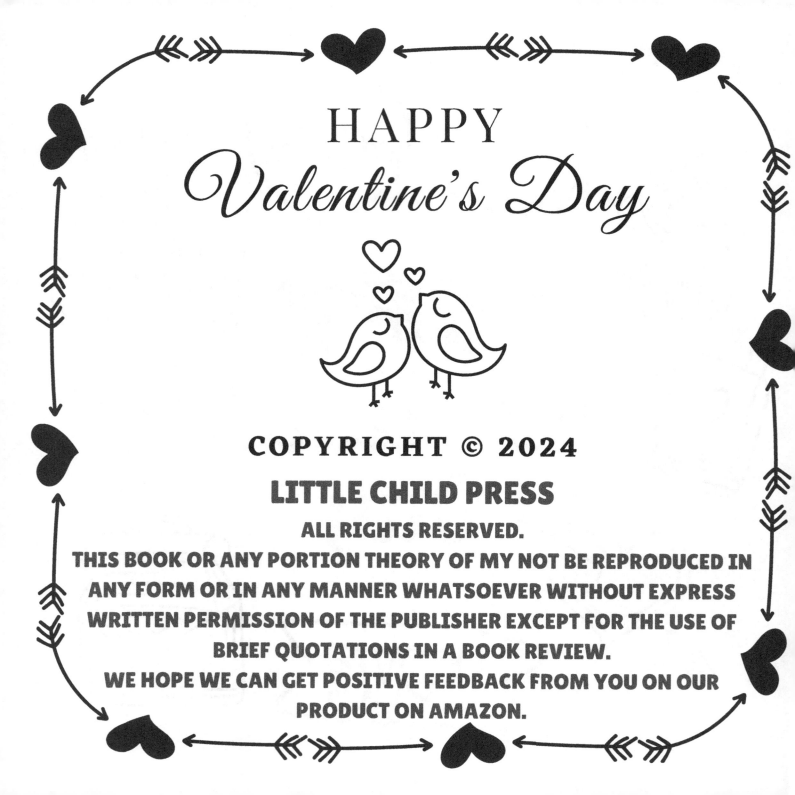

THIS BOOK
Belongs To

A is for Arrow

Let's Color

B is for
Balloons

Let's Color

C is for

Candy

Let's Color

D is for Doves

E

is for

Envelope

F

is for

Flowers

I spy with my little eye something beginning with letter...

G
is for

Gift

H is for

Heart

Let's Color

I spy with my little eye something beginning with letter...

I is for

Ice cream

Let's Color

I spy with my little eye
something beginning with letter...

J
is for

jewelry

Let's Color

I spy with my little eye
something beginning with letter...

K

Let's Color

I spy with my little eye something beginning with letter...

M

is for

Message

Let's Color

N
is for
Notebook

Let's Color

I spy with my little eye something beginning with letter...

O is for

Orange

Let's Color

P
is for
Perfume

Let's Color

I spy with my little eye
something beginning with letter...

Q is for

Queen

Let's Color

I spy with my little eye something beginning with letter...

R is for

Rings

Let's Color

I spy with my little eye something beginning with letter...

S
is for

Sweets

Let's Color

T
is for

Teddy Bear

I spy with my little eye something beginning with letter...

U
is for
Unicorn

I spy with my little eye something beginning with letter...

V

VALENTINE DAY

VALENTINE DAY

V

is for

Valentine's
Day

W is for

Writing

I spy with my little eye something beginning with letter...

X is for

XOXO

Let's Color

Y is for

yoyo

Let's Color

I spy with my little eye
something beginning with letter...

Z
is for
Zigzag

Made in the USA
Las Vegas, NV
07 January 2024

84028221R00063